J

428.1   Hanson, Joan
Ha
        Similes

Similes

as gentle as a lamb, Spin like a top...and other "LIKE" OR "AS" COMPARISONS BETWEEN UNLIKE THINGS

Sim
Joan Hanson

Published by
Lerner Publications Company
Minneapolis, Minnesota

For the Carlsons

sim•i•le (SIM-ah-lee) A figure of speech in which two unlike things are compared with the words *like* or *as*. These are examples of similes: Jack's hand is shaking like a leaf; Jane's heart is beating like a drum; Jim's face is as white as a sheet.

International Standard Book Number: 0-8225-1108-8
Library of Congress Catalog Card Number: 76-22433

4 5 6 7 8 9 10 85 84 83 82 81 80

I have a lot of friends who live in my neighborhood. Some of my friends are girls, and some are boys. Some of my friends like to play ball, and others like to read books. I have tall friends and short friends—skinny friends and fat friends. My friends are all a little different from each other and from me. Maybe that's why I like them!

My friend Mike is as stubborn as a mule.

My friend David is as quiet as a mouse.

My friend Judy swings like a monkey.

Her sister Nora can run like a deer.

Mary is always as hungry as a bear.

But Sam eats like a bird.

Diane shakes like a leaf.

Her cousin Jill grows like a weed.

Jake works like a beaver.

Jan is as slow as a turtle.

Peter sometimes gets as angry as a hornet.

His twin brother Tom is as gentle as a lamb.

Sandy is as strong as an ox.

Sarah is as graceful as a swan.

Becky sleeps like a log when she's tired.

When she wakes up, she's as nervous as a cat.

Karen is as bouncy as a ball.

Luke is as cool as a cucumber.

Larry is as happy as a lark.

Maria is as wise as an owl.

Jess can swim like a fish.

Jean leaps like a frog.

Lee spins like a top when he's excited.

But he howls like the wind when he's alone.

My friend Mark laughs like a hyena.

His little brother Nick sings like an angel.

BOOKS IN THIS SERIES

ANTONYMS
hot and cold and other
WORDS THAT ARE DIFFERENT
as night and day

MORE ANTONYMS
wild and tame and other
WORDS THAT ARE AS DIFFERENT IN MEANING
as work and play

STILL MORE ANTONYMS
together and apart and other
WORDS THAT ARE AS DIFFERENT IN MEANING
as rise and fall

HOMONYMS
hair and hare and other
WORDS THAT SOUND THE SAME
but look as different as bear and bare

MORE HOMONYMS
steak and stake and other
WORDS THAT SOUND THE SAME
but look as different as chili and chilly

STILL MORE HOMONYMS
night and knight and other
WORDS THAT SOUND THE SAME
but look as different as ball and bawl

HOMOGRAPHS
bow and bow and other
WORDS THAT LOOK THE SAME
but sound as different as sow and sow

HOMOGRAPHIC HOMOPHONES
fly and fly and other
WORDS THAT LOOK AND SOUND THE SAME
but are as different in meaning as bat and bat

British-American SYNONYMS
french fries and chips and other
WORDS THAT MEAN THE SAME THING
but look and sound
as different as truck and lorry

MORE SYNONYMS
shout and yell and other
WORDS THAT MEAN THE SAME THING
but look and sound
as different as loud and noisy

SIMILES
as gentle as a lamb, spin like a top, and other
"LIKE" OR "AS" COMPARISONS
between unlike things

MORE SIMILES
roar like a lion, as loud as thunder, and other
"LIKE" OR "AS" COMPARISONS
between unlike things

SOUND WORDS
jingle, buzz, sizzle, and other
WORDS THAT IMITATE THE SOUNDS AROUND US

MORE SOUND WORDS
munch, clack, thump, and other
WORDS THAT IMITATE THE SOUNDS AROUND US

PLURALS
mouse...mice, leaf...leaves, and other
WORDS THAT CHANGE IN NUMBER

POSSESSIVES
monkey's banana...monkeys' bananas,
thief's mask...thieves' masks, and other
WORDS THAT SHOW OWNERSHIP

LERNER PUBLICATIONS COMPANY
241 First Avenue North, Minneapolis, Minnesota 55401